PAPER FLOWERS

AND
HOW TO MAKE THEM

Illustrated

By

FLORENCE DYSON

First published in 1897

This edition is published by Old Hand Books,
an imprint of Read Books Ltd.

British Library Cataloguing-in-Publication Data
A catalogue record for this book is available
from the British Library.

www.readandcobooks.co.uk

Papercraft

Paper craft is the collection of art forms employing paper or card as the primary artistic medium for the creation of three-dimensional objects. Paper lends itself to an incredibly wide range of techniques, as it can for instance be folded, cut, glued, molded, stitched, or layered. It is the most widely used material in arts and crafts, with a long and varied history. Papermaking itself (usually by hand) is also an important paper craft, with many ramifications for its artistic, as well as other uses.

The word 'paper' derives from papyrus, the name of the ancient material manufactured from beaten reeds in Egypt, as far back as the third millennium BCE. Indeed, the earliest known example of 'paper folding' is an ancient Egyptian map, drawn on papyrus and folded into rectangular forms like a modern road map. However, it does not appear that intricate paper folding as an art form became possible until the introduction of wood-pulp based papers in China. This remarkable invention is credited to Cai Lun in the Eastern Han Dynasty, in the second century CE.

Cai Lun (c. 50 - 121 CE) was an intriguing figure. A Chinese eunuch and political official, he invented the composition for paper, along with the papermaking process in 105 CE. The tools and machinery of papermaking in modern times may be more complex, but they still employ the same ancient techniques. These techniques involve felted sheets of fibre, suspended in water, draining of the water, and then drying into a thin, matted sheet. For this invention Cai would be world-renowned posthumously, and even in his own time he was given much recognition. The papermaking process could use anything from bark, to hemp, silk, and even fishing net – though Cai Lun's exact formula has been lost. The Emperor was so pleased with his servant however, that Cai was granted an aristocratic title and great wealth.

Paper crafts are known in most societies that use paper, with certain kinds of crafts being particularly associated with specific countries or cultures. In much of the West, the term origami is used synonymously with paper folding, though the term properly only refers to the art of paper folding in Japan. Other forms of paper folding include 'Zhezhi' (Chinese paper folding), 'Jong', from Korea, and Western paper folding, such as the traditional paper boats and paper planes. Origami is certainly the most celebrated of these styles (coming from *ori* meaning 'folding' and *kami* meaning 'paper'), with the most famous model being the paper crane. In Japan, the earliest unambiguous reference to a paper model is in a short poem by Ihara Saikaku in 1680, which mentions a traditional butterfly design used during Shinto weddings.

Paper folding filled many ritual functions in Edo period Japanese culture, with noshi (ceremonial origami) attached to gifts, much like greeting cards are used today. Whilst it is the best known form of paper craft today, in early-Europe, it was almost unheard of. In the West, there was a well-developed genre of napkin-folding (which in turn influenced paper folding) which flourished during the seventeenth and eighteenth centuries. It died out however, with the introduction of porcelain, which replaced complex napkin folds as a dinner-table status symbol amongst the nobility. Despite this, some of the techniques and bases associated with the tradition continued to be a part of European culture; paper folding was a significant part of Friedrich Froebel's 'Kindergarten' method, of teaching children to learn through actively doing rather than just listening.

When Japan opened its borders in the 1860s, as part of a modernization strategy, they imported Froebel's Kindergarten system – and with it, German ideas about paperfolding. This included the ban on cuts, and the starting shape of a bicolored square. These ideas, and some of the European paper folding repertoire, were integrated into the Japanese tradition. Before this, traditional Japanese sources use a variety of starting shapes, often had cuts; and if they had colour or markings, these were added after the model was folded. In the early 1900s, Akira Yoshizawa, Kosho Uchiyama, and others began creating and recording original origami works. Akira Yoshizawa in particular was responsible for a number of innovations, such as wet-folding and the Yoshizawa–Randlett diagramming system, and his work inspired a renaissance of the art form.

In addition to the aesthetic value of paper crafts, various forms of paper crafts are used in the education of children. Paper is a relatively inexpensive medium, readily available, and easier to work with than the more complicated media typically used in the creation of three-dimensional artwork, such as ceramics, wood, and metals. It is also neater to work with than paints, dyes, and other colouring materials. Paper crafts may also be used in therapeutic settings, providing children and adults with a safe and uncomplicated creative outlet – as a base from which to express feelings.

As is evident from this very brief introduction to the art of papercraft, it is an endeavour with an extensive and absorbing history. Paper can be used to create some truly stunning works of art, whether that is by folding, sticking, or for the simple – though arguably most important role – of a simple surface on which to create. It is hoped that the current reader enjoys this book on the subject, and is inspired to undertake some paper-crafting of their own.

PAPER FLOWERS

AND

HOW TO MAKE THEM.

Introduction.

Paper Flower-making as an occupation is both educative and economical, and probably among all branches of Kinder-Garten occupations none appeals more forcibly to the intelligence and natural talent of the young.

All children love flowers; their perfume, variety of form, and bright colours are to all a source of inevitable attraction, from the tiny daisy to the most cultivated blossoms.

This natural taste of the beautiful we try to cultivate in our children, together with the training of the powers of observation and of memory, which, with deftness of touch and manipulation, are unconsciously cultivated in the above occupation.

The imitation of Nature must naturally take place from Nature itself; hence, the natural flower must be the model. Only those who have had experience in the subject can worthily describe the eagerness and fidelity with which children procure, and even search for the flower for their lesson.

Our natural pride finds pleasure in the perfection of our own work, and we find children vying seriously with Nature and exhibiting with uncontained joy the production of their skill.

The use of botanical terms for the different parts of the flower forms an introduction to Elementary Botany, and is a great aid to Nature Lessons.

These few chapters have been written as an aid for those whose happy vocation is to train these little ones, and whose great aim should be to bring happiness and life into the ordinary curriculum of school work.

At the commencement of each chapter a list of necessary materials is given, for those who, at the commencement of the course, should prefer to prepare the paper and materials. Irrespective of this, however, full instructions are given under each heading for all preparations, as after a little experience, and with a real flower as model, children can prepare—and upon this the training depends—the forms for themselves.

In all flowers the buds are generally simple, and resemble in many parts the full-blown flower; hence for them few instructions have been given; but children should be allowed to make a bud with each flower, which will form the foundation of the imitating of flowers, independently of book and other mechanical aid.

In the compilation of this little work I am much indebted to Miss Mitchell, my Head Mistress, who very kindly helped me with the diagrams of the opening chapters, and with the revision of the manuscripts.

FLORENCE DYSON.

CONTENTS.

PART I.—ELEMENTARY COURSE.

PART II.—ADVANCED COURSE.

Paper Flowers and How to Make Them.

PART I.—ELEMENTARY COURSE.

STEM MAKING.

Materials required :—

1. Length of wire 8 or 9 inches.
2. Green tissue paper 2 inches longer and ½ inch wide.

Before commencing the making of flowers, it is advisable to give a lesson on the making of stems, with a simple piece of wire and narrow strip of paper.

Lay the wire about ½ in. from left edge of paper. (Fig. 1.)

Turn the ½ in. over to the right with the whole length, holding the wire in the crease. (Fig. 2.)

Turn downwards the double paper close to the wire (Fig. 3.)

Holding the top of wire covered with paper firmly between first finger and thumb of left hand, with the same roll the wire from right to left by a movement of finger only. Keep the left hand in this position until

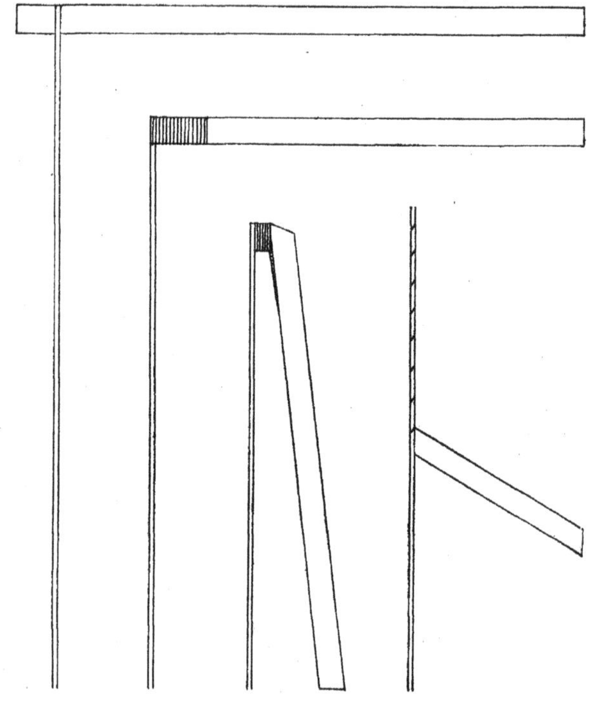

Fig. 1. Fig. 2. Fig. 3. Fig. 4.

the stem is finished; this prevents the paper unravelling. With first finger and thumb of right hand, guide the paper in its course down the stem, by holding the paper firmly round the stem. (Fig. 4.)

PAPER-BALL MAKING.

Preparation.—Take a sheet of tissue paper, which is generally oblong in form.

Fold the greater length in four, and the lesser in three. This forms almost a square. Complete square by cutting off a strip from greater side. This may be employed as a ribbon for suspension.

Fold the squares, whilst still together, into four, and curve round the corner of open edges, to form circles.

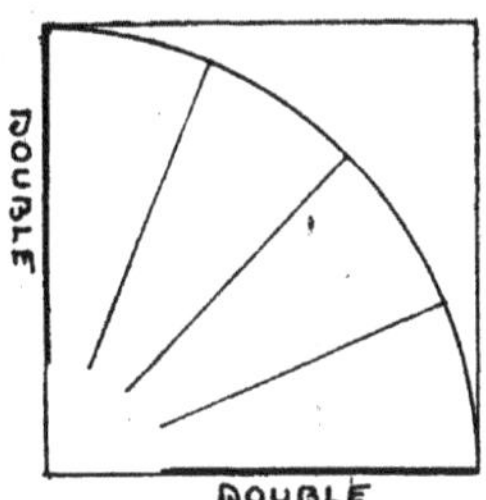

Fig. 1.

Whilst still folded, cut open the two sides of double folds, three-quarters down.

Divide the quadrant into four by making three cuts, each three-quarters of the distance to the centre.

These preliminaries serve for almost all balls.

Snow Balls.

Materials required :—

1. One and a half sheets of tissue paper.
2. Length of wire 6 ins.

Take eighteen circles, that is, cut up 1½ sheets of paper in the manner described.

Before opening out, round the end of each division.

Open out the circles. Take each point, and whilst holding in left hand, twist the end with thumb and forefinger. (Fig. 3.)

Care must be taken not to crumple the paper, but to give, if possible, the round form of forefinger.

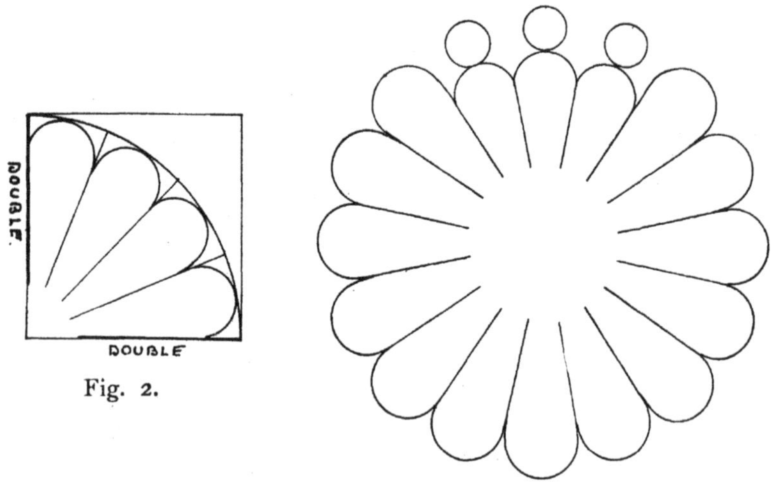

Fig. 2.

Fig. 3.

When all are prepared, take a length of wire about 10 ins. Make a knot at one end with a small piece of paper. Then thread on all the circles through the centre.

Draw all tightly together, and retain them so by making a little loop in the wire, at the same time attaching the ribbon. Shake out gently.

Dahlia Balls.

Materials required :—

1. A half-sheet of pale pink tissue paper
2. A half-sheet of rose tissue paper
3. A half-sheet of green tissue paper
4. A length of wire of 6 ins.

(Items 1–3: for 3 balls.)

Prepare as for Snow Balls, cutting circles half the size, and in three shades of paper—green, rose, and pale pink are pretty.

A dozen circles are sufficient—four of each colour. Arrange in sprays of five or seven, all the ribbons being of different lengths.

Cactus Balls.

Materials required :—

1. One and a half sheets of tissue paper.
2. Thin slate pencil.
3. Six inches of wire.

Prepare the same number of circles as for Snow Balls. Cut into points, but do not round the ends. Take a slate or thin programme pencil. Roll each division round the pencil. Touch the end with gum. Fold over. Draw out the pencil very gently, so that the paper retains its open form.

Thread on a length of wire, and attach a ribbon.

Porcupine Balls.

Materials required :—

1. One and a half sheets of tissue paper.
2. Ordinary lead pencil.
3. Six inches of wire.

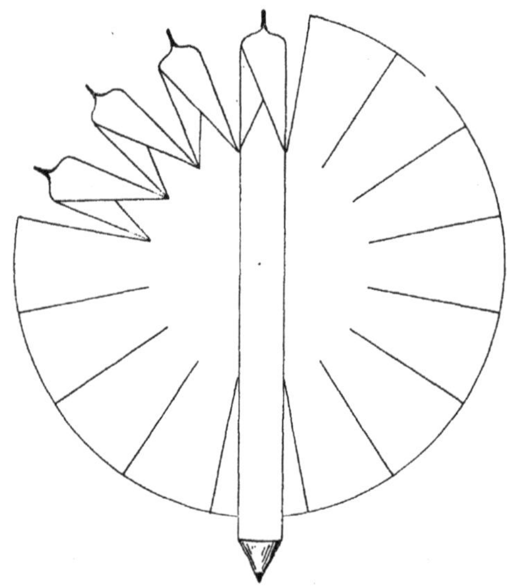

Prepare exactly as for Cactus Balls. In rolling round the pencil, use the flat end. Lay the pencil on the paper, leaving a quarter of an inch over the end. Whilst holding in left hand, twist the overhanging quarter inch into a neat little head. Thread on a wire as above.

Peony Balls.

Materials required :—

1. Two sheets of tissue paper.
2. Six inches of wire.

In these balls, cut the paper into squares of any desirable size, say—four inches. Open out. Take each square separately, by the extreme centre, in right hand, and crinkle, by drawing several times between the third and fourth fingers of left hand. Slightly open, and crease again.

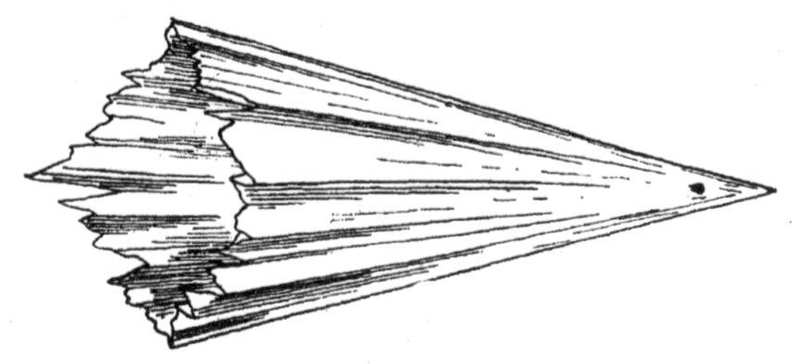

Two sheets of paper, cut into squares of this given size, will be required.

When all are crinkled, pass a wire through the central tip marked by a dot.

When all are threaded in a long string, fasten together the wire, by twisting one round the other, so as to draw all the threaded papers tightly together.

The above balls may be made in all colours, and if different shades of the same colour, tastefully combined, are used, they make an extremely pretty decoration.

ROSES.

Materials required:—

1. Half a sheet of pink, red, yellow, or white tissue paper (two roses).
2. Length of wire of 12 ins.
3. Strip of green tissue paper, 7 ins. by ½ in. for stem.

Method of Preparing Paper.—This flower is made from rounds of paper. Supply each child with half a sheet of plain tissue paper, and give following directions :—

Lay paper on desk with length running horizontally, and short sides right and left. Hold paper at corners, and fold short sides together in three. (Fig. 1.)

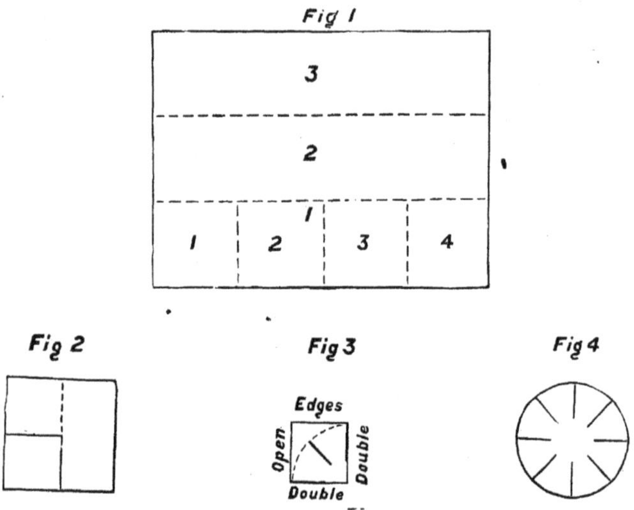

Fold length across in half, crease, and fold again into quarters. Fold this square again across and down (Fig. 2.)

Lay on desk with double fold to right and front, and draw with pencil a quadrant round open edges. (Fig. 3.)

Cut round pencilled curve, three-quarters of way down the folded sides, and three-quarters way down centre of each quadrant—open circle. (Fig. 4.)

Forming of Rose.—Each round has been cut into eight petals, and as twelve rounds have been prepared, these will make two roses, five rounds being necessary for one rose.

The two corners of each petal are curled on the knitting needle, by twisting the corners round the needle with the finger and thumb. (Fig. 5.)

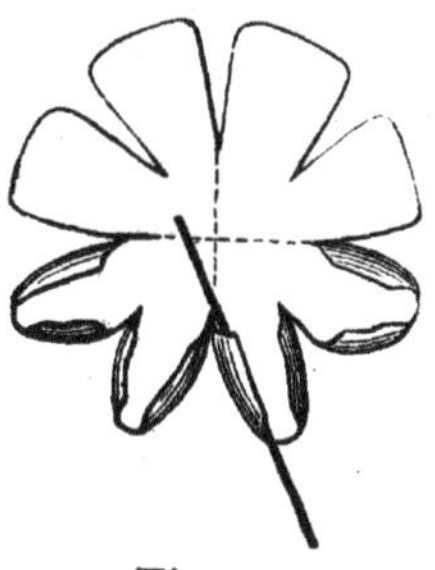

Fig. 5.

In this way prepare five rounds or circles.

Arrangement.—A piece of fine wire, twice the length of the stem, is required. This is doubled in two, and the two points passed through a round a little distance from each other. Thread on two of the curled rounds, and squeeze them up to represent partly closed centre of flower, curled petals to face centre of flower. If desirable, other curled petals might be threaded to curl back. This is simply a matter of choice.

Thread on the remaining three rounds, taking care that petals are not evenly arranged, as that destroys the natural appearance.

Fastening and Stem.—The flower is now drawn together by squeezing the paper round by the wire, and while holding it in left hand, twist one wire round the lower part with the right hand to make rose firm. The flower is then completed by twisting a narrow strip of green paper round two wires for stem.

If necessary, the flower stems may be touched with gum, but if green paper is put round bottom of flower, wire twisted over it, two wires put together, and paper carefully wrapped to the bottom, the flower is quite firm.

PINKS.

Materials required :—

1. Strip of pink tissue paper 16 ins. by 2 ins. for petals.
2. An eight inch length of wire for stem.
3. A piece of green tissue paper 2 ins. by $\frac{3}{4}$ in for calyx.
4. A strip of green tissue paper 7 ins. by $\frac{1}{2}$ in. for stem.

Method of preparing Paper.—For this flower a strip of paper the length of the sheet and 2 inches in width is required. This must be placed end to end, and folded several times until only about half an inch wide, that giving an oblong 2 ins. by $\frac{1}{2}$ in.

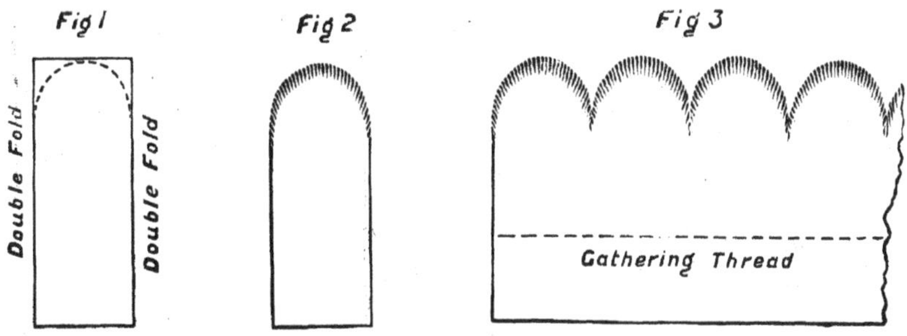

Very little cutting is required for this flower. Begin rather more than half-way up strip, and round the top nicely, taking care to cut off very little from the sides. (Fig. 1.)

Fringing.—The rounded edge must now be fringed finely. Begin to fringe from middle of curve down both sides respectively, so as to give an equal appearance. (Fig. 2.) Open out. (Fig. 3.)

Forming of Flower.—The length of paper must be gathered. It can be drawn together with the fingers in folds, and worked round in the shape of a flower. For infants the easier method is to gather with needle and thread. Draw up carefully, and twist the thread round the paper on a line with the gathering thread to hold all together. A piece of wire, rather longer than required stem, is twisted twice round the flower on the top of the cotton, and the remainder forms the stem. The bottom of petals are covered with green paper to form the calyx about $\frac{3}{4}$ in., and a narrow strip is wrapped round the wire for stem.

CHRYSANTHEMUM.

Materials required :—

1. Strip of pink, yellow, brown, or white tissue paper 24 ins. by 4 ins.
2. A piece of wire 8 ins. long.
3. A piece of green paper 1 in. by 2 ins. for calyx.
4. A strip of green tissue paper 7 ins. long and ½ in. wide.

Method of preparing Paper.—This flower is made of suitable coloured tissue paper. Cut a strip 24 ins. x 4 ins. Fold length from end to end into about six or eight thicknesses. This is simply to facilitate cutting. Cut into a fringe from the edge about 2½ ins. up the 4-in. side, and each fringe about ⅛ in. in width. (Fig. 1.) Open out.

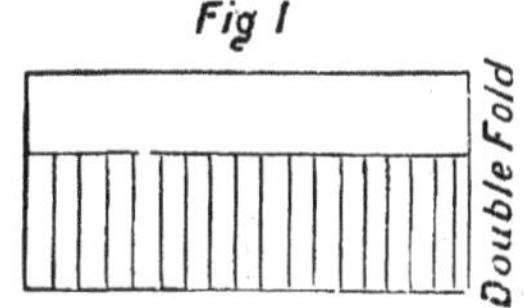

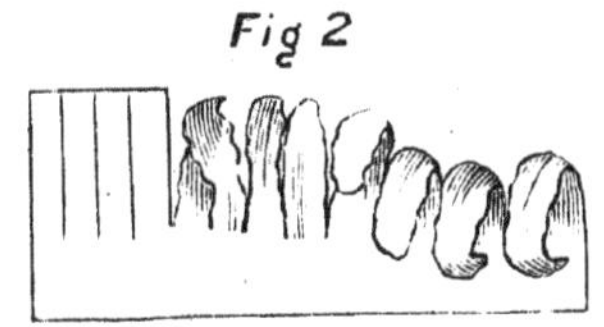

Curling Petals.—Each fringe requires curling. This is done with a knitting needle. The cut paper must be placed on something rough and thick ; the dress of the child is best. Lay the paper on one knee, with the fringe away from the child. Lay knitting needle almost parallel on centre of each fringe, and with a little pressure draw the needle towards the person from the edge of the fringe. Do each fringe in this way.

Arrangement of Flower.—After all are curled, the

flower is made up. Roll about one-sixth of the paper up tightly to form partly closed centre. Then wind the remainder round loosely.

The flower may be made with the petals turning either towards centre or outside. A piece of wire, suitable length for stem, is twisted round the paper at the bottom of the flower, and the stem is finished off in the usual way with green paper.

DOUBLE OR GARDEN POPPY.

Materials required :—

1. A strip of red crêpe paper 18 ins. long and 4 ins. wide.
2. A piece of wire 12 ins. long for stem.
3. A boot-button, or black bead for capsule.
4. A piece of green tissue paper for stem, 7 ins. by $\frac{1}{2}$ in.

Fig 1

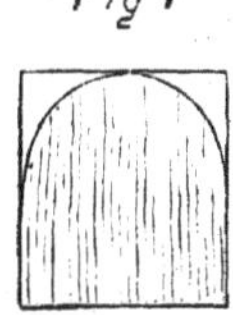

Fig 2

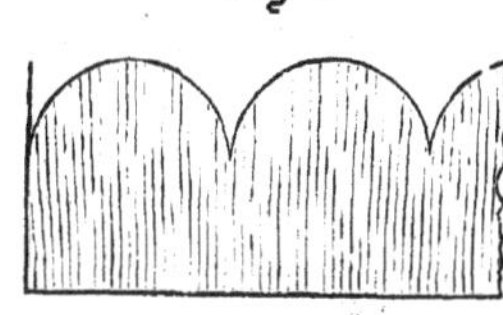

Preparing Paper.—Cut a length about 18 ins. by 4 ins. of crêpe paper. Fold until this is about 3 ins. by 4 ins. Round top of oblong as for Pinks. (Fig 1.) Open out. (Fig 2.)

Fig 3

A piece of wire twice the length of stem must be threaded on the bead, and twisted round close to it, andfour or five times down the stem. (Fig. 3.)

Forming of Flower.—The strip of paper forming the petals must now be arranged round the head of the bead. Hold stem and bead in left hand. Place one end of petals round stem, and arrange round the stem in layers, gathering slightly while wrapping round. Fasten bottom of petals securely round stem close up to bead with a short length of wire.

Calyx and stem are made in the same way as for Pinks.

Note.—The paper must be cut with the grain running from top to bottom of the 4-in. strip.

CARNATION.

Materials required :—

1. Crimson crêpe paper 10 ins. long, 2 ins. wide.
2. 18 ins. of white thread, or,
   Piece of white crêpe paper, 2 ins. by 1½ ins., fringed and twisted.
3. Length of wire 8 ins.
4. Piece of green tissue paper 2 ins. by 1¼ ins. for calyx.
5. Strip of green tissue paper 8 ins. by ½ in. for stem.

Method of preparing Paper.—Take a strip of crinkled paper, 10 ins. by 2 ins. Fold lengthwise four times. The paper will now be sixteen thicknesses. The top is now slightly rounded. This must be done as sparingly as possible, simply curving off the two corners, and cutting down each side about half-way. This forms the petals. The curved top must now be finely pinked. (Fig. 1.)

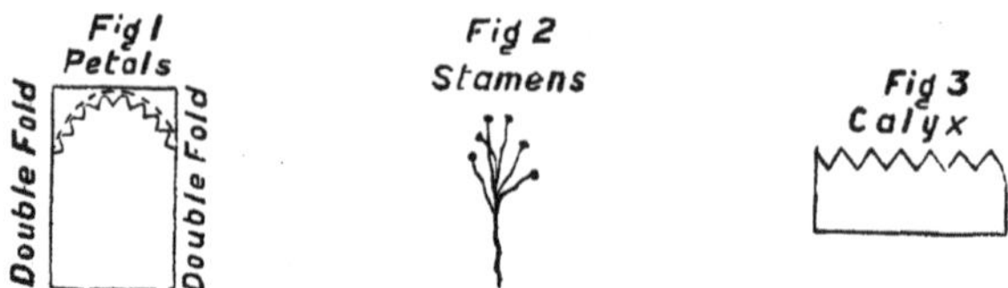

Stamens.—These are formed of six or eight lengths of thread, about 2 to 3 ins., with a small knot at one end. These must be dipped in gum and dried. (Fig. 2.)

Calyx.—The green paper for covering the calyx must be about 2 ins. in length and 1¼ ins. in width. This requires to be folded, and the top cut into six points. (Fig. 3.)

Arrangement of Flower.—Attach gummed centres with a piece of wire about 8 ins. in length, which will be long enough also for the stem.

Round these centres commence arranging the length of petals, rather closely and quite straight at first for about three rows, then gradually fuller, allowing the fulness to increase to the outer layer.

Twist the wire round the bottom of petals to make all secure. This lower part, over which the wire has been twisted, must be covered with the green paper already prepared, and fastened securely by a touch of gum, to form the calyx. The stem must be covered with a narrow strip of green paper.

The outer petals of the flower need to be taken separately in the fingers, and opened out a little, so as to slightly fall over.

This flower may also be made in pink or white paper.

Those made of white paper might have the pinked edges slightly tipped with red ink.

Paper Flowers and How to Make Them.

PART II.—ADVANCED COURSE.

FUCHSIA.

Materials required :—

1. A piece of white crêpe paper 1 in. by 2 ins. (along grain) for stamens.
2. A piece of white crêpe paper 4 ins. by ¼ in. for pistil.
3. A piece of red tissue paper 1½ ins. by 4 ins. for petals.
4. A piece of white crêpe paper 2½ ins. by 2½ ins. for sepals.
5. A length of wire 7 ins.
6. A strip of white crêpe paper 1½ ins. by 1 in. for calyx.
7. A strip of green tissue paper 8 ins. by ½ in. for stem.

Preparation and Arrangement.—The stamens and pistil are made from white crêpe paper. There are four stamens, for which a piece 1 in. by 2 ins. is required. Fold in four, making oblong 2 ins. by ¼ in. Cut down the folded edges 1¾ ins. Roll between first finger and thumb of right hand. (Fig. 1.)

The pistil must be made in the same way, but twice the length of the stamens; therefore it requires a strip of paper 4 ins. by ¼ in. Arrange the stamens round the pistil, giving a twist to the paper, which will bind them together. (Fig. 2.)

They may also be made of thick crochet cotton, knotted at the ends to represent anthers and stigma; or of wire covered with white tissue paper, like a stem, with a tiny roll at the end of each.

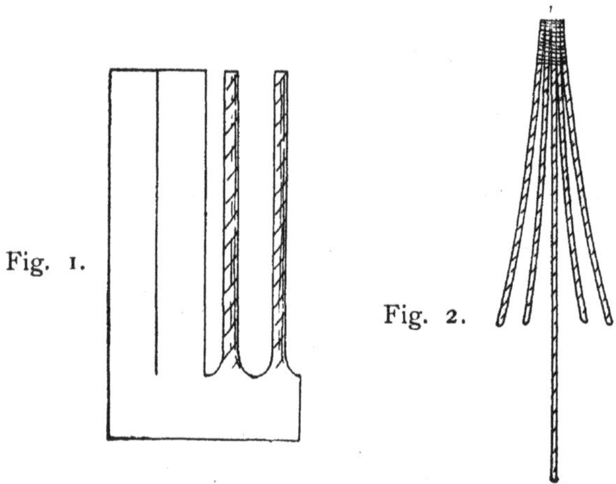
Fig. 1.
Fig. 2.

Petals.—Take a piece of red tissue paper 1½ ins. by 4 ins. Fold into four, making oblong 1½ ins. by 1 in. This is the size of each petal. Fold again, making 1½ ins. by ½ in. As it is now folded, the two sides of the petals may be cut together. With lead pencil curve the corner ⅓ from end of open edges. From the base of the petals, ⅓ from the double fold, make a compound curve to meet the first. (Fig. 3.) Cut out.

Arrange the four petals round the stamens, pleating the bases, and attaching with a piece of fine wire, leaving a long end to attach the sepals and serve for stem later on. (Fig. 4.)

Sepals.—For the four sepals, take white crêpe paper, 2½ ins. by 2½ ins. Fold in four, making oblong, 2½ ins. by ¾ in. nearly. Fold again in two. From top corner of double fold, curve out a lanceolate-shaped leaf, leaving ½ in. at the base. Cut and arrange, alternating with the petals. Attach with wire.

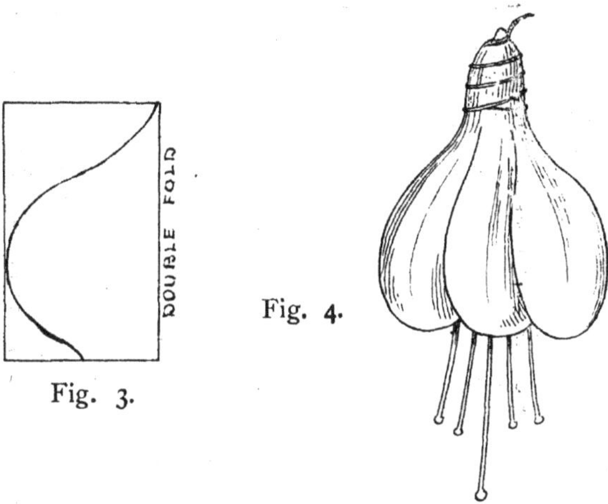

Fig. 3.

Fig. 4.

The sepals may be curved backwards when the flower is finished. (Fig. 5.)

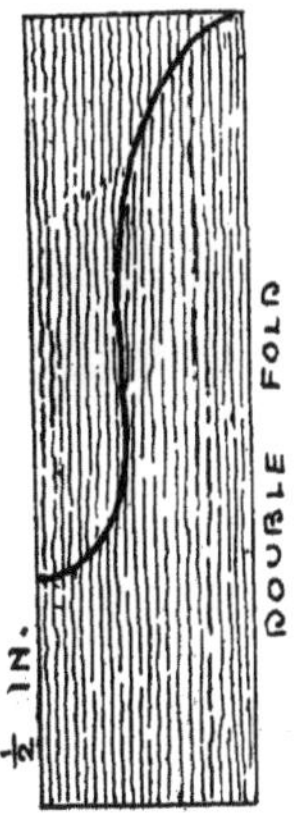

Fig. 5.

To cover wire and paper, etc., wrap round a piece of white paper 1½ ins. by 1 in. This in the natural flower is a continuation of the sepals forming the calyx.

Now cover the stem with green paper as in other flowers.

Take each sepal between the first finger and thumb of right hand, and curve backwards a little, opening the folds of the paper at the base of the curve with the end of the thumb.

Thin wire is the best for this flower, as the weight of the flower will then give the natural curve to the stem. If thick wire be used, the stem must be bent.

For double Fuchsia, use eight or more petals, of white or purple tissue paper, and make the sepals of red crêpe paper, with surrounding band red also.

WHITE LILY.

Materials required :—

1. Seven pieces of wire 5 ins. long for stamens and pistil.
2. Seven pieces of yellow tissue paper 6 ins. long by ½ in.
3. A piece of crêpe paper 10 ins. by 4½ ins.
4. A piece of wire 8 ins. long for stem.
5. A strip of green paper 9 ins. by ½ in. for stem.
6. Four-inch square of green crêpe paper for four foliage leaves.

Preparation and Arrangement.—Six stamens and a pistil are required. Therefore cut seven pieces of wire

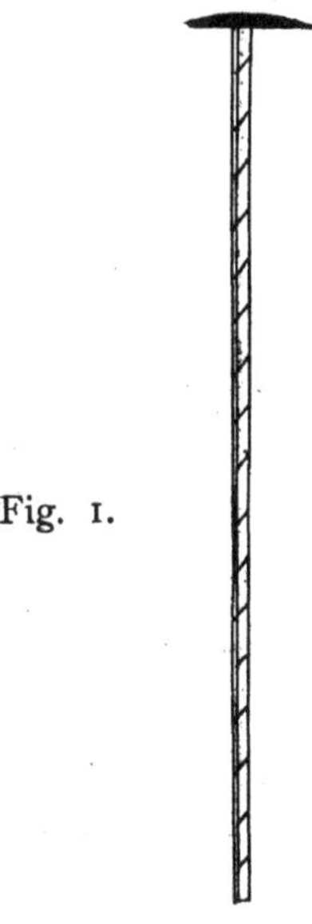

Fig. 1.

5 ins. long. Take narrow strip of yellow tissue paper and twist round the wire as for stems.

To represent the heavy anther lobes, fold the wire in two little folds at one end, twisting it back again to the middle so as to form letter T. (Fig. 1.) A piece of double Berlin wool gummed on the top has a very natural effect.

To form the stigma of the pistil, continue twisting the yellow paper several times so as to form a head.

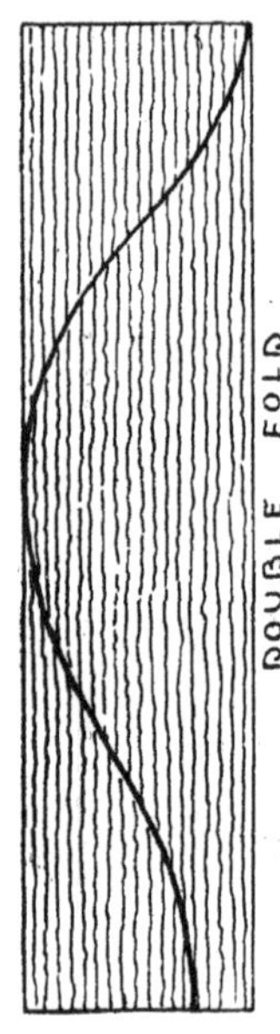

Arrange the stamens in a circle round the pistil, and twist round a piece of wire to hold them in position.

Petals.—A piece of crêpe paper 10 ins. by 4½ ins. is required, with the grain along the 4½ ins. Fold in two, and again in three, so as to have six petals, each 4½ ins. by 1⅔ ins. Fold again so as to cut both sides together.

Begin at the top corner of double fold, making a decided point. Make a compound curve terminating at the edge of the paper in the middle of the petal. At

$\frac{1}{3}$ from double fold at base of petal make a deeper but similar curve to meet the other. Arrange the petals alternately, in two rows of threes, around the stamens, making a little pleat at the base of each, and twisting round the wire at same time. Twist round the stem a narrow strip of green paper.

Take the extreme tip of each petal between first finger and thumb of left hand, and with the tip of first finger and thumb of right hand open out the petal about $\frac{1}{2}$ in. from the edge to the middle of the leaf. Then, holding the tip in right hand, give a similar curve to the left side of the petal. Arrange the stamens so that each is opposite a petal, and, if desired, dot the petals with red ink or brown chalk.

From green crêpe paper, foliage leaves may be cut, and arranged alternately along the stem.

ARUM LILY.

Materials required :—

1. A 5-in. square of writing paper, or, } for tongue.
   A 10-in. square of tissue paper }
2. A piece of crêpe paper (white) 8 ins. by 8 ins.
3. A length of wire 7 ins.
4. A strip of green tissue paper 8 ins. long and ½ in. wide.

Preparation and Arrangement.—The centre or tongue of lily must be made of yellow paper, and, when finished,

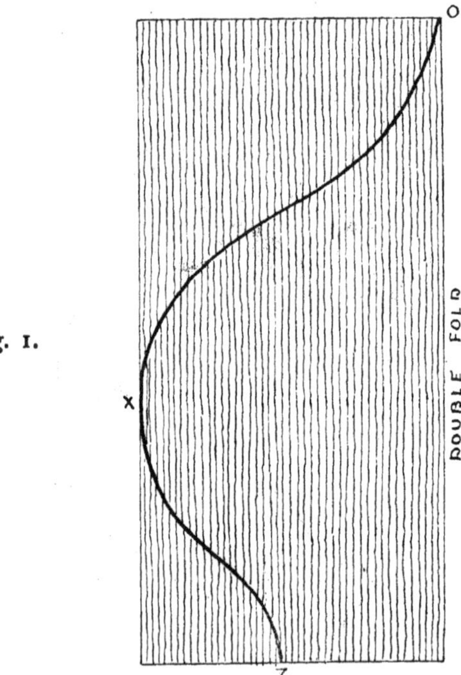

Fig. 1.

5½ ins. long. It may be made of a length of wire covered with cotton wool, in the form of a thick somewhat pointed finger. Cover evenly with yellow paper, gumming the edges neatly, and give the whole a slight bend backwards.

Rough tissue paper rolled loosely in the form of a pointed finger, and lightly wired so as to bend in the direction of the flower, may also be used.

Spathe.—Take a piece of crêpe paper, 8 ins. by 8 ins. Fold in two, making oblong 8 ins. by 4 ins., with grain along 8 ins.

Lay on the desk with double fold to right hand. About midway of the 8-in. side of open edges make a dot, X. Half-way along the 4-in. base make another, *Z*.

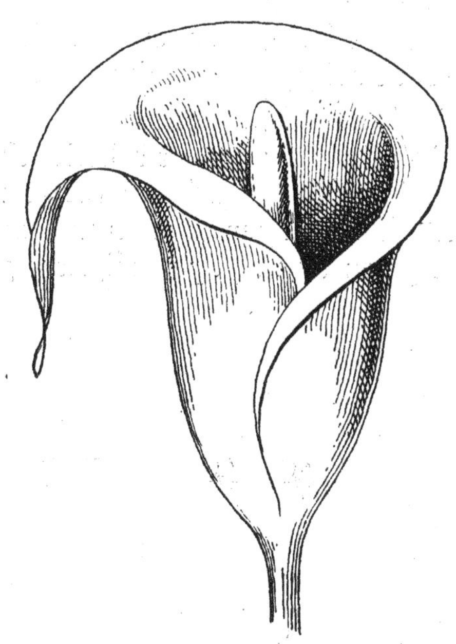

From top right-hand corner make a deep curve, leaving a long and decided point, and gradually round off to X. From *Z* make a compound curve to X. (Fig. 1.) Cut

Open, and touch at upper surface of left edge with gum, three-quarters of the distance from *Z* to X.

Wrap the right edge over the left, forming a cup, the two edges just meeting at *Z*, but overlapping almost 1½ ins. at X.

Now, taking the wide upper edge between the thumb and first finger of each hand, and beginning at the point, almost an inch from the edge, with the finger of right hand under the spathe, smooth out the paper towards the gummed edges. This is to give the necessary curve to the flower, and upon this being well done depends its success.

When both sides have been curved place the tongue in the centre, attaching it to the base of spathe by twisting round a piece of wire.

With the first finger open out a little the base of the cup from the inside. To thicken the stem, roll round loosely waste tissue paper or cotton wool, afterwards covering with green tissue paper, slightly gummed.

BLUEBELL.

Materials required :—

1. A strip of blue tissue paper $7\frac{1}{2}$ ins. by 1 in.
2. Pencil or penholder.
3. Length of fine wire 14 ins.
4. Strip of green tissue paper 14 ins. by $\frac{1}{2}$ in.
5. Piece of green crêpe paper 3 ins. by 6 ins. (grain).

Materials.—Blue and green tissue paper, green crêpe paper for leaves, wire, pencil or penholder.

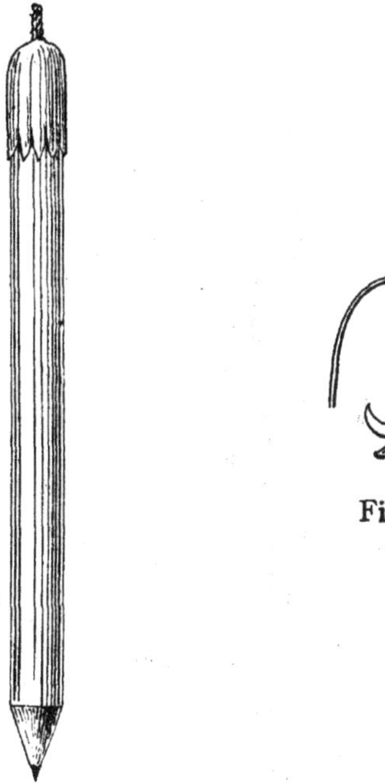

Fig. 1.

Fig. 2.

Preparation and Arrangement.—Take a strip of blue tissue paper about an inch in width. Fold many times and fringe or notch one end to a depth of $\frac{1}{4}$ in.

Open out, and curl back the fringes by passing between the thumb of right hand and the blade of a penknife or scissors held in the same hand.

Cut the paper into lengths of 1½ ins. Take one piece and twist round the end of a pencil, leaving a little more than ⅛ in. of unfringed end over the end of the pencil,

which must be twisted tightly; then with the twisted end draw from off the pencil. (Fig. 1.) Twist round a piece of very fine wire about 1½ ins. in length.

Calyx and Stem.—Cut a strip of green tissue paper 2 ins. by ½ in. Cut one end into six points, which will serve as calyx. Place round the flower, covering the wired portion, and continue twisting round the tiny stem. (Fig. 2.)

Prepare four or five flowers, varying in size, by using different sized pencils. To the smallest attach a long piece of fine wire, which will serve as stem.

Twist round a very fine piece of green paper for about one inch of stem. Then attach another flower, and continue wrapping round the paper.

Cut long narrow leaves of crêpe paper, varying from 4 ins. to 6 ins. in length and generally ½ in. in widest part. Arrange around the bottom of the stem.

Bend the flower stalk and pedicels in a drooping form natural to the flower.

CARNATION.

Materials required :—

1. Six squares of red, white, pale yellow, or variegated tissue paper, of 3 ins. side.
2. Slate or lead pencil.
3. A piece of wire $3\frac{1}{2}$ ins. long or two filaments of a feather.
4. A piece of wire 7 ins. long for stem.
5. A strip of green tissue paper $1\frac{1}{4}$ ins. square for calyx.
6. A strip of green tissue paper 8 ins. long and 1 in. wide for stem covering.

The petals are cut from circles of about 3 ins. in diameter. As five or six are required for each flower, many may be cut together.

Take any sized piece of paper. Fold as often as necessary until it forms squares of 3 ins. Take several

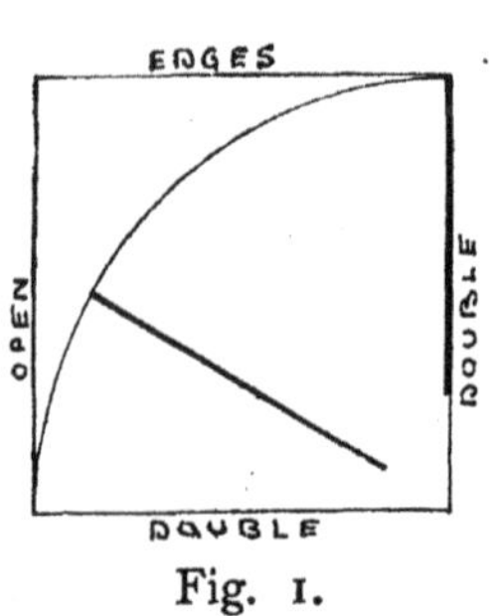

Fig. 1.

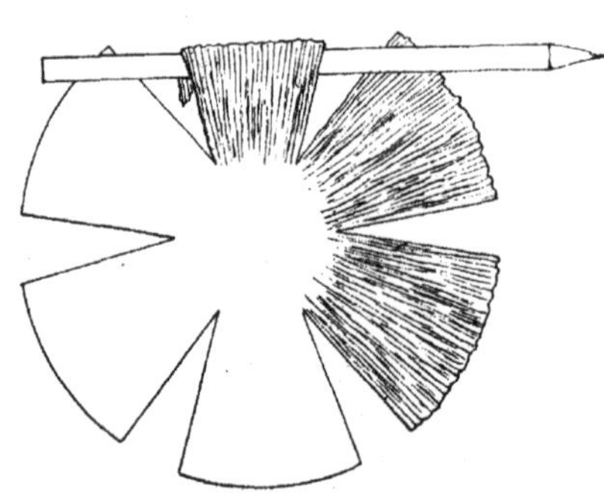
Fig. 2.

squares. Fold into quarters, and round off the open edges to form circles. In order to have six petals in each, cut open the folded edges on *one* side three-quarters of way down, and the same distance one-third from the double fold of the other side. (Fig. 1.) Open out.

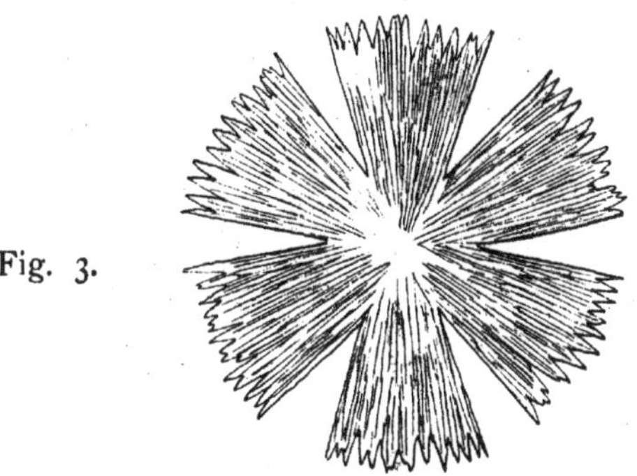

Fig. 3.

Take a thin lead pencil or penholder, and place each petal one by one over it. Whilst holding firmly in right hand, work the paper towards the right with thumb and forefinger of left hand, forming the tiniest

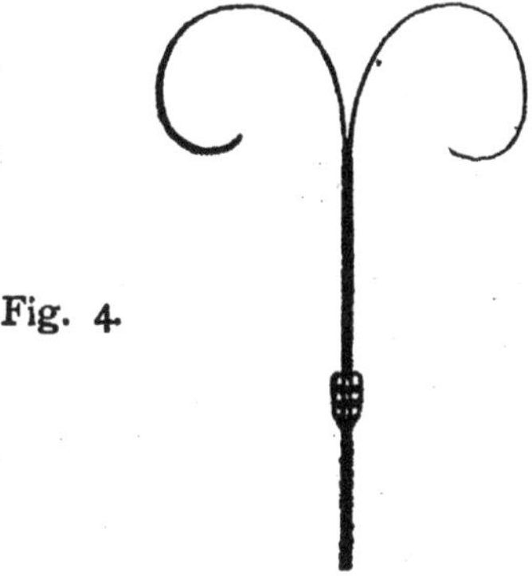

Fig. 4.

creases, and thus giving it the appearance of crinkled paper. If not well creased the first time, open slightly and crease again. When all are crinkled, cut and point the edges in various ways. (Fig. 3.)

Pistil.—To represent the hooked styles, a piece of wire 3½ ins. long finely covered with white tissue paper, and the two ends curved outwards, may be used, to the middle of which the wire for stem must be attached. A prettier and more effective method is to take a good-sized white feather of a fowl or duck and strip off two filaments. With a small piece of paper to hold them firmly, place them together, and twist round the wire. Then pass each one between the thumb and blade of scissors or penknife, to curl outwards. (Fig. 4.)

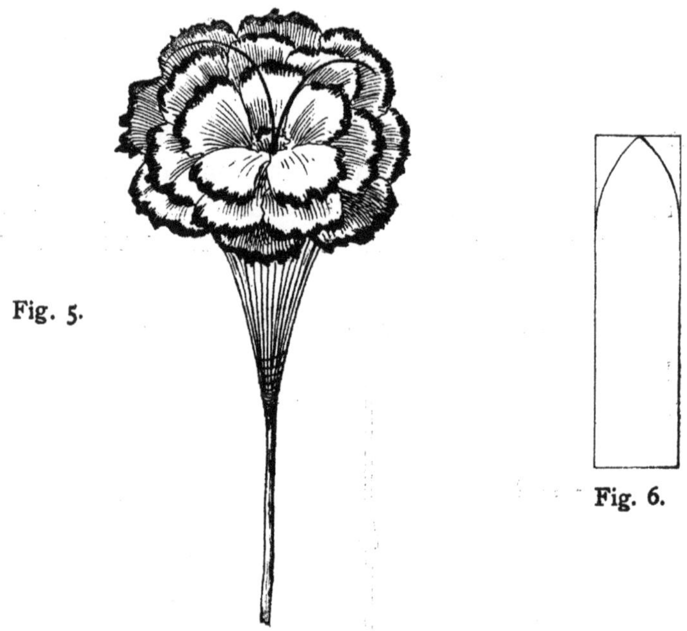

Fig. 5.

Fig. 6.

Arrangement.—Pass the wire of stem through five circles of petals, so that the petals of each layer alternate with those of the layer above. Draw all up together, and twist a small piece of wire round the bases. (Fig. 5.) Touch the edges of petalswith red ink

Calyx.—Take a piece of green tissue paper from 1 in. to 1¼ ins. in length and width.

Fold lengthways in two, and then in three.

Point the top, nearly half-way down, to form the sepals. (Fig. 6.) Open out, and place round lower part of flower, twisting securely, or attaching with gum.

Twist a narow strip of paper round the stem, placing long pointed leaves, cut from crinkled paper, at intervals.

MOSS ROSE.

Materials required :—

1. A strip of pale pink tissue paper 12 ins. by $3\frac{1}{2}$ ins.
2. A knitting needle.
3. A length of wire of 7 ins.
4. A piece of green tissue paper 2 ins. square for calyx,
5. A strip of green tissue paper 8 ins. long and $\frac{1}{2}$ in. wide.

Preparation of Paper.—Cut off a strip of paper from an ordinary sheet $3\frac{1}{2}$ ins. wide.

Fold repeatedly until an oblong is formed $3\frac{1}{2}$ ins. by 2 ins.

Cut open all the double folds $2\frac{1}{2}$ ins. down. Open out.

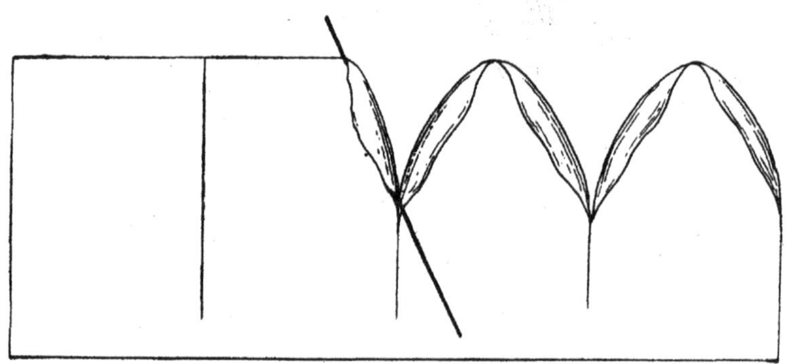

Fig. 1.

The first three petals may be cut again in order to have smaller ones for centre of rose.

The two corners of each petal must be curled over a knitting needle, holding the needle between first finger and thumb of right hand, and turning between first finger and thumb of left. (Fig. 1.)

Forming of Rose.—Begin with the small petals. Tear off from the strip each petal as required.

Take one petal in right hand, and gathering up the base tightly between first finger and thumb, take the extreme middle tip of the petal between finger and thumb of left hand and stretch firmly, when the petal will assume a very natural form.

The curled side of the petal must be to the outside.

Now take a second petal, and wrapping half way round the first, gather and treat in the same way, and so on with all the petals, gathering less at the base as the rose increases in size, until a desired size is obtained.

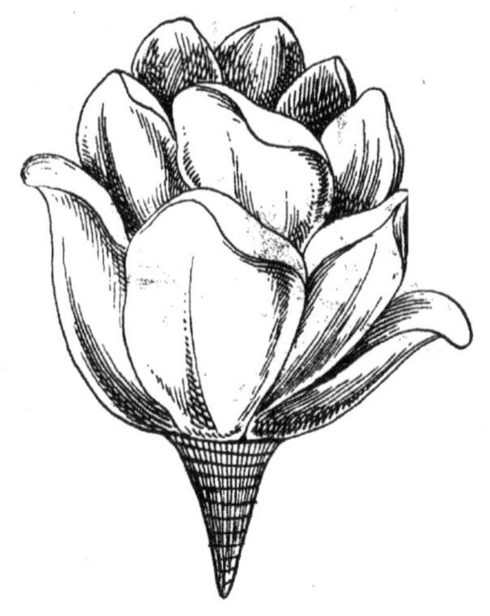

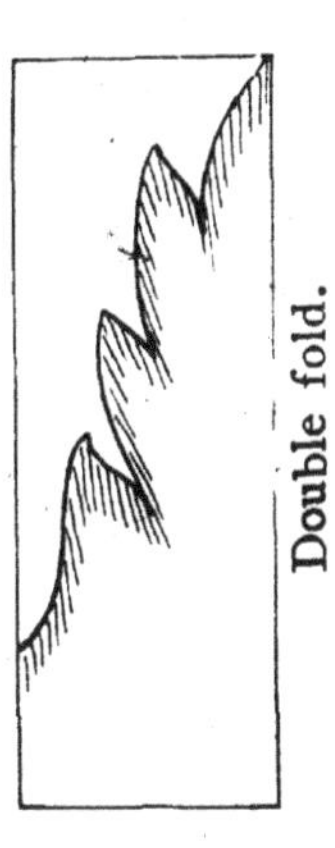

Fig. 2.

Twist a piece of wire round the base, leaving an end long enough for stem. (Fig. 2.)

Calyx.—Take a piece of green tissue paper 2 ins. by 2 ins. Fold into four, making 2 ins. by $\frac{1}{2}$ in. This is the size of the sepals. Fold again, making 2 ins. by $\frac{1}{4}$ in.

From upper point of double fold, curve out a long, much-indented leaf, leaving $\frac{1}{3}$ from the bottom uncut.

While still folded, fringe finely the cut edges.

Arrange round the lower part of flower, attaching the edges with a little gum. Slightly touch the back of three of the sepals to make them adhere to the rose.

Twist green paper round the stem, which also may be fringed along one edge.

Three petals with calyx of same size as rose, and gummed quite up to the tips, makes a pretty bud.

CACTUS DAHLIA.

Materials required :—

1. Five squares of red, yellow, brown, or white tissue paper of 4 ins.
2. A long fine-pointed pencil.
3. A length of wire of 7 ins. for stem.
4. A piece of green tissue paper 2 ins. by 1 in. for calyx.
5. A strip of green tissue paper 8 ins. by ½ in. for stem.
6. Gum, or flour paste, or starch paste.

Preparation of Paper.—Fold paper in squares of 4 ins. Take five and fold into four. With lead pencil draw quadrant round open edges to form circles.

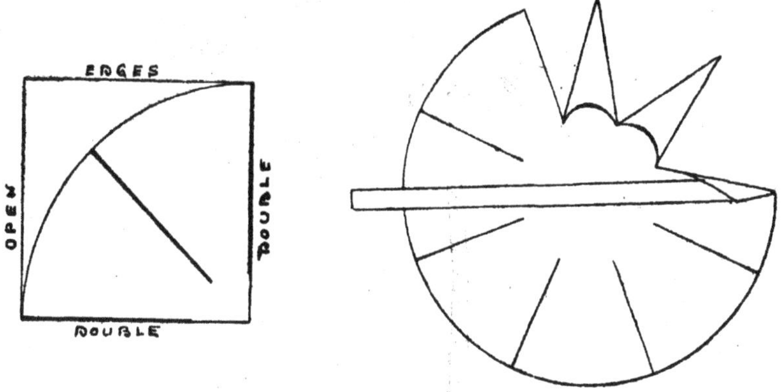

Cut round the pencilled curve, and three-quarters down the folded sides and middle of quadrant. Open the circles. Each consists of eight petals. Of one, cut each petal again, making sixteen. This will serve for the middle one.

Take a fine lead pencil with a long, well-sharpened point, and twist each petal tightly round the point in the form of a spike. (Fig. 2.) In this way prepare five circles.

Draw up the circle of small petals tightly from the base, and twist round a piece of wire. Pass the end through the four other circles, drawing together a small portion of the base. Twist round the wire to hold all together in position.

Take a piece of green tissue paper 1 in. by 2 ins. Fold in eight, making 1 in. by $\frac{1}{4}$ in. Shape the small end into a point $\frac{1}{4}$ in. in depth. Arrange round base of flower, and complete by covering the stem with green paper.

If the folding edge of petal is slightly touched with gum at the terminating point only whilst folding round the pencils, these dahlias remain in good condition a very long time.

WILD ROSE, APPLE BLOSSOM, AND BUTTERCUP.

Materials required :—

1. A piece of paper 1 in. wide and 2 ins. long, bright yellow, for stamens.
2. A circle of pale pink or yellow tissue paper of 3 ins. diameter.
3. A circle of green tissue paper of 3ins.
4. A length of wire of 6 ins. for stem.
5. A strip of green tissue paper 7 ins. by ½ in. for stem.

Materials.—Tissue paper, pale pink and white for rose and apple, yellow for buttercup, fine wire.

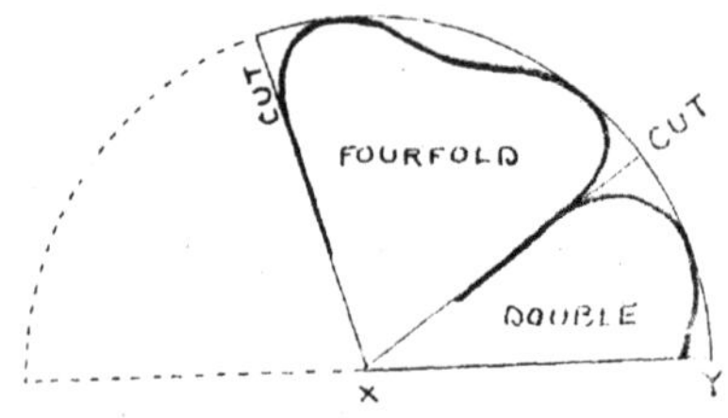

Fig. 1.

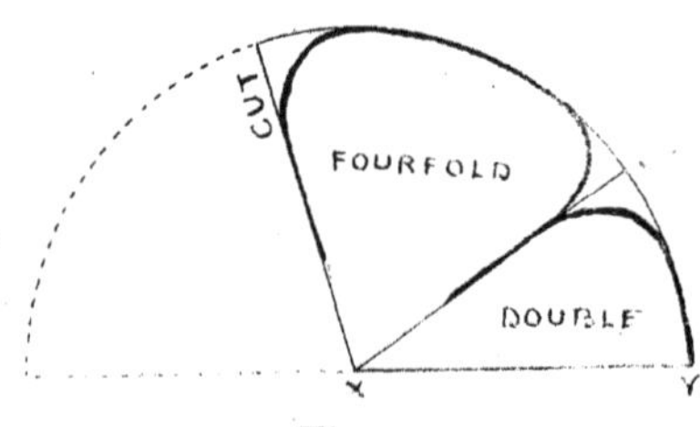

Fig. 2.

Preparation.—The three flowers have a somewhat similar size, form, and arrangement.

For each set of stamens take a length of bright yellow crêpe paper 1 in. wide and 2 ins. long. Fold, and fringe one two-inch side extremely fine in half-inch fringes.

Petals.—These are cut from circles of 3 ins. For rose and buttercup fold so as to form five petals (Fig. 1), and cut nearly to the centre on each side of fourfold, taking care not to cut the double fold at X Y. Round off the corners slightly, and for rose and apple the middle of each petal also, but not so for buttercup. (Fig. 2.)

For apple blossom fold to form six petals, as they are slightly narrower. Shape like rose petals, afterwards cutting out so as to leave five for flower.

Calyx.—Cut circles of green tissue paper of 3 ins. Fold into six. Fold again. (Fig. 3.)

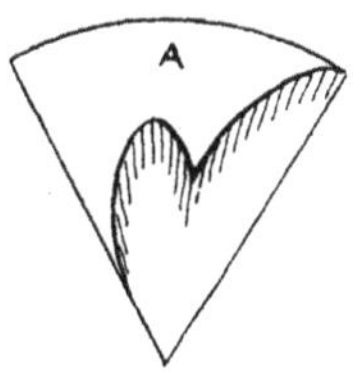

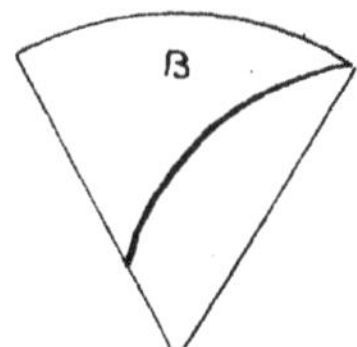

Fig. 3.

(*a*) For rose begin from the top corner of one side and cut a two-pointed edge. Arriving nearly at the centre (*a*), fringe slightly.

(*b*) For apple and buttercup make a single curve. Open, and cut out one sepal. Five only are required.

Arrangement.—Gather up the bases of the stamens into a tiny bundle. Place a circle of petals and sepals together (alternating). Arrange the stamens in the middle, drawing a very small portion of the bases together, and, whilst holding in left hand, arrange a little the petals and sepals.

Twist round a piece of fine wire to serve as stem, and cover with a narrow strip of paper. Curl the petals towards the centre with blade of penknife or scissors.

Occasionally replace a pink petal of rose and apple by a white one. Curl some petals at a single point, another in the middle or at both ends.

IRIS.

Materials required :—

1. A piece of purple, white, or yellow crêpe paper 12 ins. by 4 ins., the grain along the 4 ins.
2. Six lengths of wire of 4 ins. for petals.
3. Gum or needle and black thread.
4. A length of yellow double Berlin wool of 9 ins.
5. An 8-in. length of same.
6. A length of wire, very strong, of 8 ins.
7. A strip of green tissue paper 9 ins. by $\frac{1}{2}$ in.

Preparation.—The petals are in two sets of three, the upper slightly smaller than the lower.

Cut six petals 4 ins. by 2 ins., the grain of paper along 4 ins. Fold forming oblong 4 ins. by 1 in.

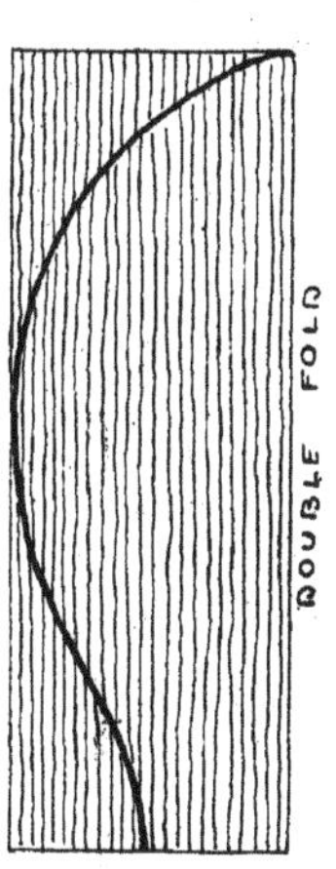

Fig. 1.

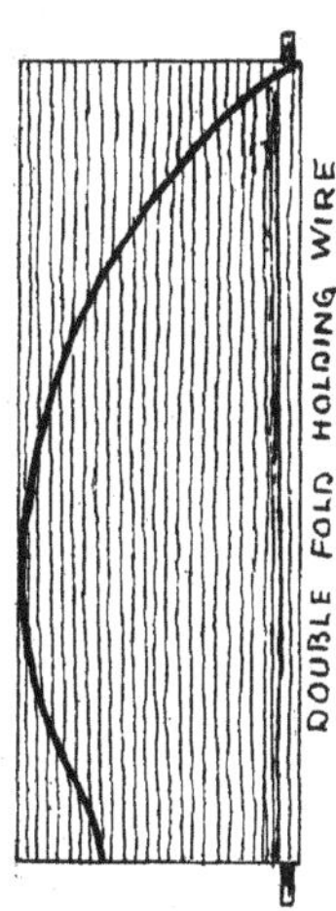

Fig. 2.

Draw a full round curve from top corner of double fold to middle of open edge, and curve a little towards the base.

Each petal must be wired. Cut six lengths of wire of four inches. Cover well with gum, and lay in the centre of each petal, adding more gum if necessary to make the paper adhere round the wire.

This enables the petal to retain its curved form. If preferred the wire may be sewn in the paper like a piping cord. (Fig. 2.) Open out and flatten the paper, so that the wire lies in a little pleat in the middle of the leaf. From three petals cut off a quarter of an inch from width and length, in order that they may serve for upper petals.

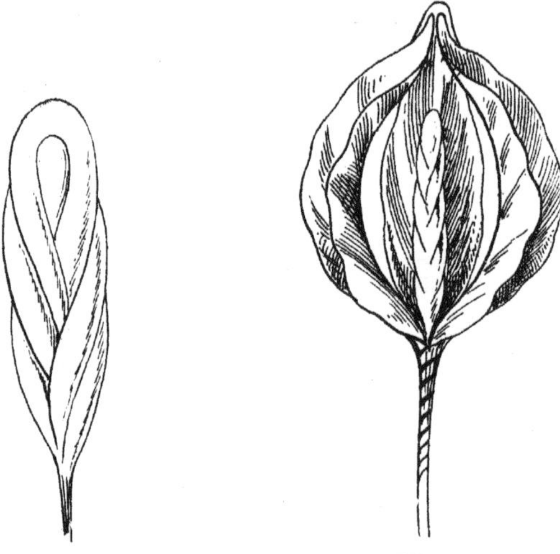

Fig. 3. Fig. 4.

Cut six lengths of wool $1\frac{1}{2}$ ins., and point one end of each. Touch slightly one side with gum, and place one on each petal, beginning at the middle of the base with unpointed end on the side on which the wire was laid.

Take an 8-inch length of wool ; double it ; twist four or five times and double again ; attach the two ends with a piece of wire.

Take three petals and straighten out the edges by passing between first finger and thumb of both hands.

Arrange round the prepared centre, with the side bearing the wool to the outside, pleating the bases where necessary. Attach with wire. Bend evenly towards the middle until the tips of the petals meet. (Fig. 4.)

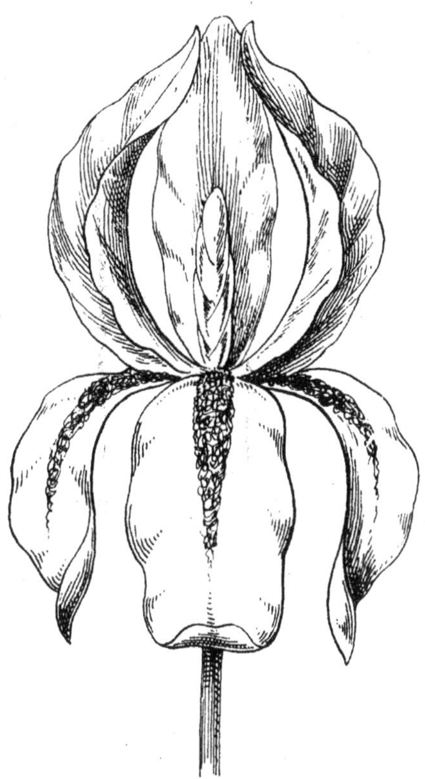

Now arrange the three outer petals round the bases of the three upper ones, with the wool uppermost, and alternating with the others.

Twist round the wire and attach a length of very strong wire to serve as stem. Cover the stem with green paper.

Open out the edges of the lower petals as in the upper ones, and gently curve them downwards.

Cut large leaves from green crêpe paper, varying from 12 in. to 16 in. in length, and from 2 in. to 3 in. in width, tapering suddenly to a point at one end.

Three flowers with about a dozen leaves form an extremely pretty plant.

These are amongst the most effective of all paper flowers, and always remain in good condition.

BEGONIA.

Materials required :—

1. Two pieces of prettily coloured crêpe paper 1½ ins. by 1 in.
2. Two pieces of same colour, 1 in. by ¾ in.
3. A piece of bright yellow crêpe paper 4 ins. by 1 in.
4. A length of wire of 6 ins. for stem.
5. A strip of green tissue paper, 8 ins. by ½ in.

Method of Preparation.—Four petals are required, two being larger than the others, though of the same form.

For the larger prepare two pieces of paper 1½ ins. by 1 in., and for the smaller two pieces 1 in. by ¾ in. Fold in two with grain along greater length, and round off the top open-edged corner, curving in a little towards the base. (Fig. 1.)

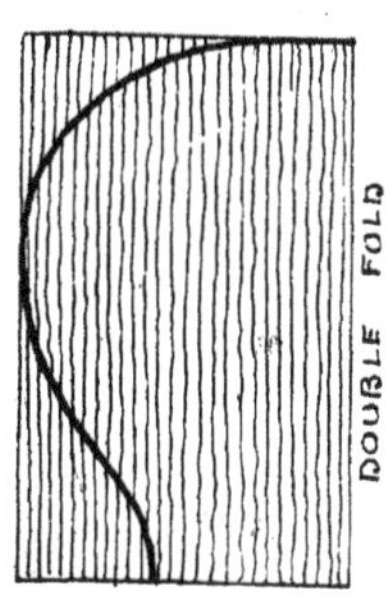

Fig. 1.

Stamens.—Take a strip of bright yellow paper 4 ins. by 1 in., and fringe finely ½ in. in length. Roll up into a little rosette, and arrange round it the petals, the two large and the two small opposite each other.

As no calyx is required, cover the stem with green paper. Then, taking each petal between first finger and thumb, open out the paper a little, giving each petal its full rounded form, and an occasional turn.

Arrange in sprays. These flowers may be made in any size or colour. With yellow Berlin wool for stamens a pretty effect may be produced, especially if previously knitted and unravelled.

PENTSTEMON.

Materials required :—

1. A piece of red or violet coloured crêpe paper, 3 ins. by 2½ ins., grain along 2½ ins.
2. A piece of white crêpe paper 2½ ins. by 1¼ ins. (grain along 2½ ins.)
3. A piece of green tissue paper 1½ ins. by 3 in. wide.
4. A length of wire of 7 ins.
5. A strip of green tissue paper 8 ins. by ½ in.
6. Gum.

Preparation.—A piece of coloured crêpe paper 3 ins. by 2½ ins. is required for the corolla, with grain along 2½ ins. Fold, making oblong 2½ ins. by 1½ ins. From top corner of open edges mark down ½ in. Beginning

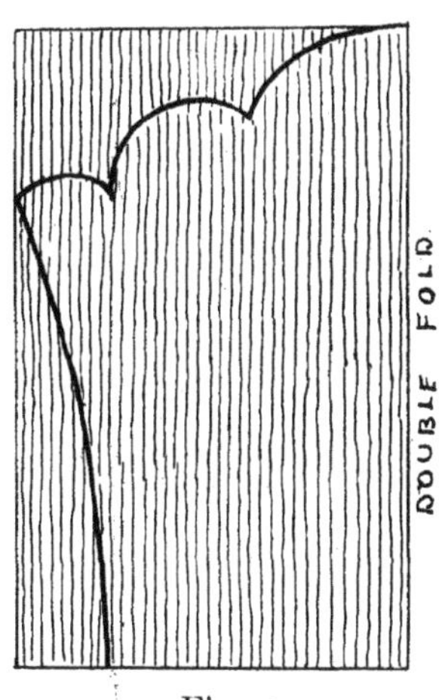

Fig. 1.

at the top of double fold, descend in three curves to the half-inch mark, each curve decreasing a little in size. (Fig. 1.)

From the last curve which meets the edge, continue to the base slanting inwards ½ in. Gum together the edges to form cup.

Fig. 2

Stamens.—The five stamens are of the same length as the corolla. Take a piece of white crêpe paper 2½ ins. by 1¼ ins. Cut into five fringes 2 ins. long, and roll them between finger and thumb. Make the pistil similar to the stamens, but ¼ in. longer, and

arrange the stamens round it, twisting a piece of fine wire round the bases. Place in the middle of the corolla, drawing the base of the latter around that of the stamens, and again twisting round the wire.

Calyx.—Take a piece of tissue paper 1½ ins. long, and ¾ in. wide. Fold the length into five, and cut one end into ¼ in. points. Gum together the edges to form a cup, and place round the base of the corolla. Attach with wire. (Fig. 2.)

Cover the stem with green paper. Take each tiny lobe, and curve backwards, by smoothing out the paper over the point of first finger. Place the first finger inside the flower and also open out the corolla at the base. Give it a full and round form.

Make several flowers, increasing and decreasing the size, and arrange many on one stem, beginning with the smallest. As in the case of snapdragon, with which all children are familiar, the flowers are arranged on one side of the stem only.

CANTERBURY BELL.

Materials required :—

1. A piece of blue or white crêpe paper 2¼ ins. by 3 ins. (grain along 2¼ ins.)
2. A piece of white crêpe paper 2¼ ins. by 1¼ ins. for stamens.
3. Five pieces of green crêpe paper 1½ ins. long, 1 in. wide for sepals.
4. A length of wire of 7 ins. for stem.
5. A strip of green tissue paper 8 ins. by ½ in. for stem.
6. Gum.

Preparation and Arrangement.—Cut the paper for corolla in pieces of 2¼ ins. by 3 ins.

Fold, and cut the top edge of 3 ins. into six points of ¼ in. depth.

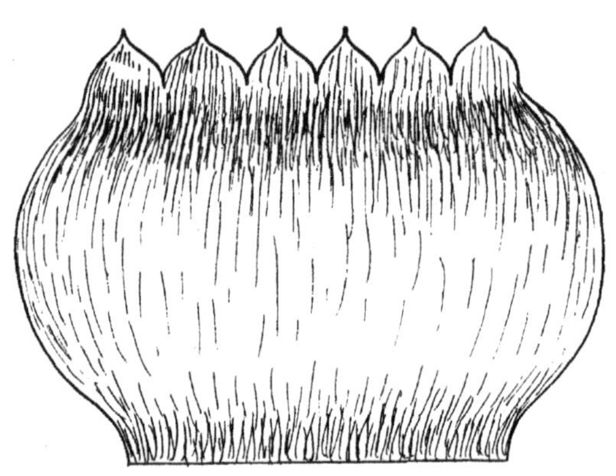

Fig. 1

This flower bulges out much in the middle of the corolla. To obtain this form, straighten out the paper of this part by passing between the first finger and thumb of both hands, taking care not to straighten at all at the base, nor at the neck, below the pointed edge, which must be kept as small as possible. Turn back the points by curving over the tips of the fingers. Gum together the edges wrapping over the first and sixth points, five lobes only are required in the flower. (Fig. 1.)

Stamens.—A strip of white crêpe paper, 2¼ ins. by 1¼ ins. will just cut five stamens of an equal length with the corolla. A pistil must be cut 2½ ins. long by ¼ in. wide.

Roll each between first finger and thumb, and, gathering the base round the pistil, twist round the wire. Place in the centre of the corolla already gummed, and attach all with wire. (Fig. 2.)

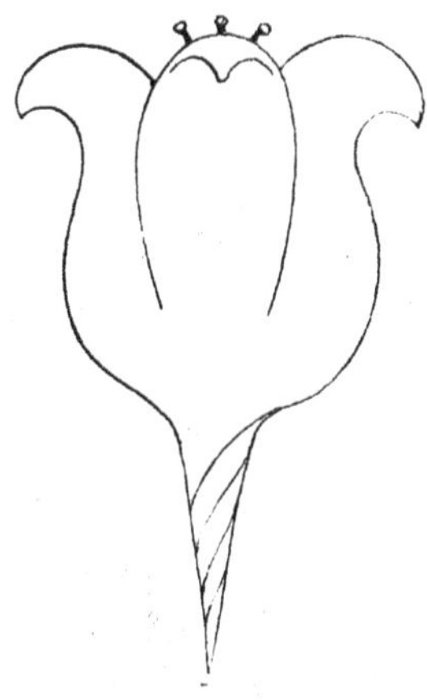

Fig. 2.

Calyx.—The calyx consists of five fairly large foliaceous sepals.

Cut from green crêpe paper pieces of 1½ ins. by 1 in.

Fold in two in order to cut both sides together. From top corner of double fold make a compound curve to the middle edge of the leaf, and continue to the middle of the base. (Fig. 3.)

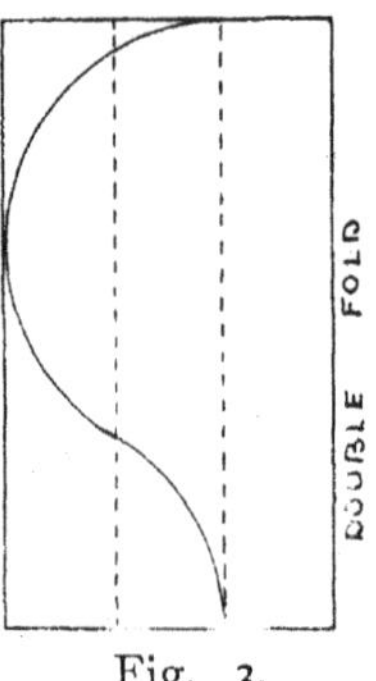

Fig. 3.

Arrange round the base of the corolla, and complete by twisting round the stem a narrow strip of green paper.

DAFFODILS.

Materials required :—

1. A piece of orange crêpe paper 1¾ ins. long and 1 in. wide for cup, or 2 ins. by 1¼ ins.
2. A piece of pale lemon crêpe paper 4½ ins. long and 2 ins. deep for petals (grain along 2 ins.).
3. A piece of orange crêpe paper, or brownish tissue paper as used for wrapping parcels, 2 ins. by 1½ in., for sheath.
4. Strip of green tissue paper for stem, 8 ins. by ½ in.
5. A piece of orange crêpe paper 2 ins. by 1½ ins. for stamens (as in Fuchsia).
6. Three or four pieces of green crêpe paper 5-7 ins. long and ½ in. wide, for leaves.
7. Gum for Teacher.

Cup.—Cut lengths of orange paper 1¾ in. long and 1 in. wide. Slope off ¼ in from each end, and cut along one long side in curves, and fold back from dotted line. (Fig. 1.) Gum edges "*a*" and "*b*" (Fig. 1) very lightly (dissolved dextrine or clear starch is preferable, as it does not darken the paper), fold back curves again, and set to dry.

Fig 1

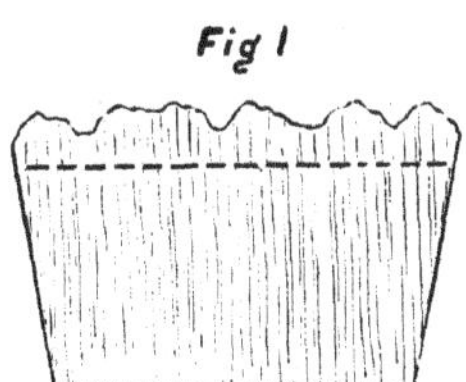

Stamens.—These may be prepared in two ways. Pale yellow cotton may be cut in lengths, somewhat longer than cup, and knotted at the end to represent pistil, not necessarily all the same length.

Six of these will be required for one flower, and they may be dipped in gum, put together at the bottom, while wet, and set to dry. (Fig. 2.)

Another method is to twist very narrow strips of paper, and slightly roll one end into a knot for pistil.

Petals.—Pale lemon. Cut six leaves about 2 ins. long and ¾ in. wide, and shape (Fig. 3), and one of orange for the sheath.

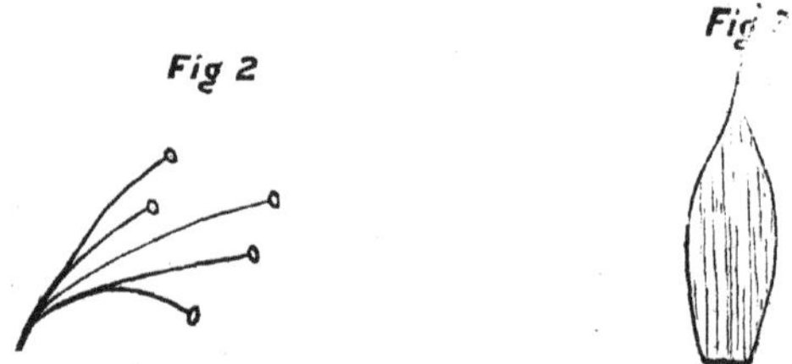

Leaves.—Cut from dark green paper two or three strips about 5 ins. long and ½ in. wide, shape at top like daffodil leaves.

Arrangement.—Fasten centre of a long length of wire through bunch of stamens and also through cup of the flower, draw the cup together at the lower end, press down into cup shape, taking care not to stretch paper. Wrap one end of wire firmly round stamens and cup. (Fig. 4.) It is now advisable to touch lightly bottom of cup with gum; put on one petal, drawing bottom of leaf narrow, and wrap with cotton. Place another petal half resting over last and wrap again. Continue this until five petals are set round and wrapped with cotton. Touch twisted cotton with gum, and wrap strip of plain green paper round, then bend wrapped stem about ½ in. down.

Take orange leaf for stem, gather bottom in fingers and place it at the bead, wrap it with cotton, and over it wrap green paper. The wire stem must now be wrapped with green paper, and leaves put in vase with single flowers.

Fig. 4.

Leaves and flowers might be mounted into sprays by twisting about three leaves at intervals, with about three flowers on to one stem with cotton, touch with gum, and finally wrap with green paper.

MARGUERITE DAISY.

Materials required :—

1. A strip of white or yellow crêpe paper 7 ins. by $1\frac{1}{2}$ ins. for petals.
2. A piece of green tissue paper 2 ins. by 1 in. for calyx.
3. A yard of yellow or brown wool for centre; or a strip of yellow crêpe paper 6 ins. long with one edge finely fringed.
4. Wire 12 ins. long for stem.
5. Needle and thread.
6. A strip of green tissue paper half-an-inch by 7 ins. for stem.

Method of preparation.—For this flower a strip of white crêpe paper is required 7 ins. by $1\frac{1}{2}$ ins. This is

Fig I

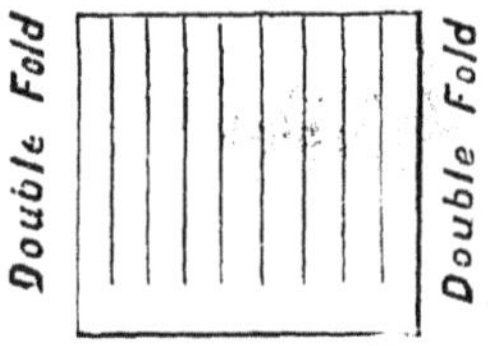

Double Fold

Double Fold

folded in four, and the petals then cut $1\frac{1}{4}$ ins. down, and the width of an ordinary daisy petal. (Fig. 1.)

Fig 2
Round or Pointed Petals

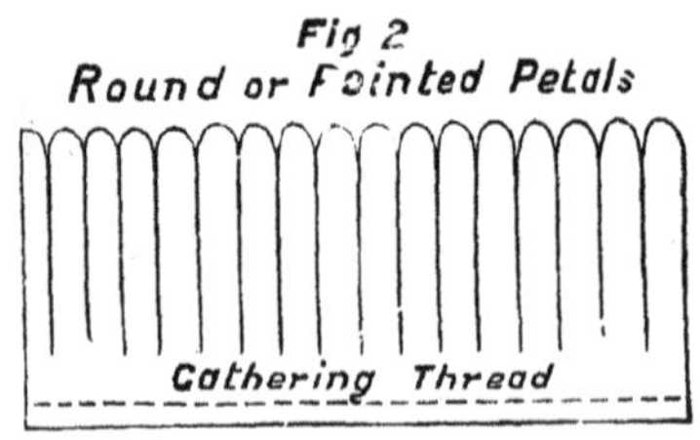

Each point must now be cut round or pointed.

Open out. (Fig. 2.)

Gather with needle and thread along length as shown by dotted line (Fig. 2), and not at the bottom of the petals.

Centre of Flower.—This is made of yellow wool folded several times. A piece of wire, twice the length of stalk is cut, and at the middle is placed round the wool and twisted to hold it in position. (Fig. 3*a*.) The centre is then cut round, and the ends shaved off until it is the shape of a daisy centre. It is more natural to be round and slightly flat. (Fig. 3*b*.)

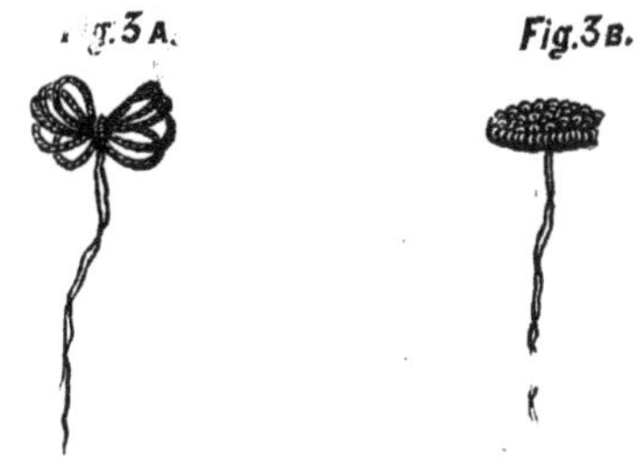

Arrangement.—The paper length of petals is now drawn up on the gathering thread, and placed round under the centre piece, to which it is attached by twisting the cotton round five or six times, and fastening off with a few stitches.

The petals require pushing back or flattening, and arranging evenly all round.

A strip of green tissue paper is twisted round the gathered edges of the white paper, and continued down the stem.

These daisies look very pretty when made in yellow paper with brown centres. Their sizes may be varied by cutting the paper shorter and narrower, or longer and wider.

SUNFLOWER.

Materials required :—

1. 5 circles of 6 in. diameter of golden-yellow paper or a strip of crêpe 3 ins. by 14 ins. with petals cut as in Marguerite.
2. 4 circles of yellow tissue paper, diameter 2 ins., and 8 circles of brown tissue paper, diameter 2 ins.
3. A piece of stout wire 8 ins. long.
4. A piece of green tissue paper 2 ins. by 1 in. for calyx.
5. A strip of green tissue paper 8 ins. by ½ in. for stem.

Method of preparing Paper.—Leaves.—The sunflower is made from circles of paper, in two sizes; the larger for the outer petals made of yellow paper, and the centre from smaller circles, both of brown and yellow.

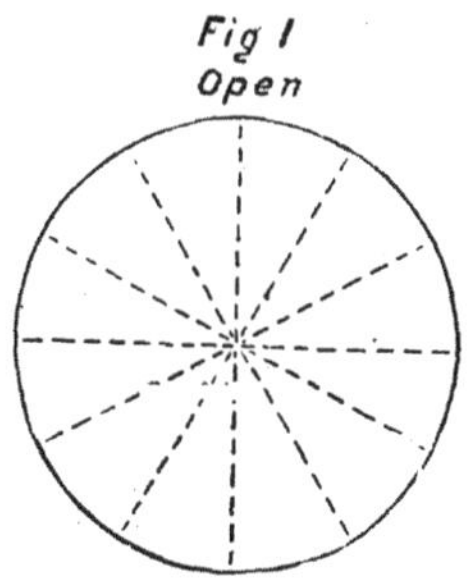

The larger circles are about 6 ins. in diameter. Cut these out by the method previously described for Roses. Five of these are required for each flower, so they may be cut together.

Take five circles and fold in four, and again into three. (Figs. 1 and 2.)

While thus folded, this must be cut from the centre point in a curve three-quarters of the length down each side (*dotted line*, Fig. 2.)

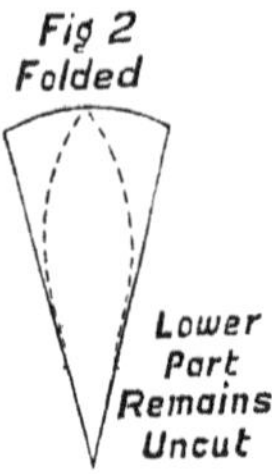

Centre.—The centre circles are 2 ins. in diameter. Twelve of these are required, 4 yellow and 8 brown. These must be fringed all round ½ in. in length, and one-tenth of an inch in width. (Fig. 3.)

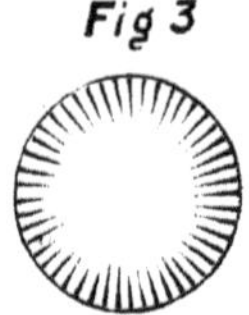

Arrangement.—A piece of wire the length of the stem is knotted at one end. This knot is hidden in the centre. The small circles are threaded in the following order, viz. :—Two brown and one yellow. Repeat until all are threaded. A piece of paper folded round the stem close to the flower will form the calyx, or more strictly, involucre.

This must be fastened with a little gum, or a small piece of wire twisted round.

The calyx and stem must now be covered with green paper.

Two widths of paper are best for the stem, one wide enough to form the calyx, and the other for the stem proper, very wide indeed. This is the case with al flowers having a deep calyx.

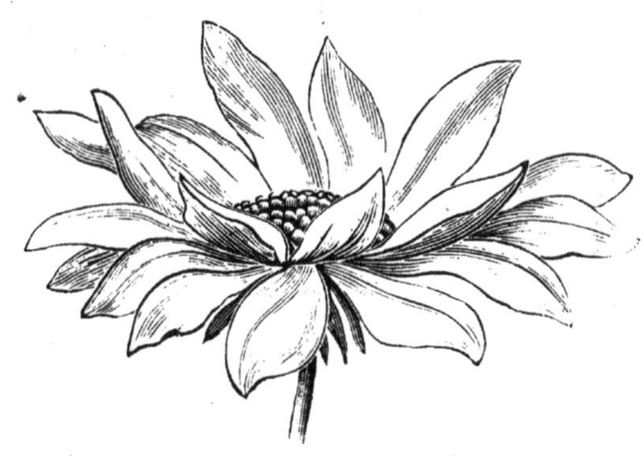

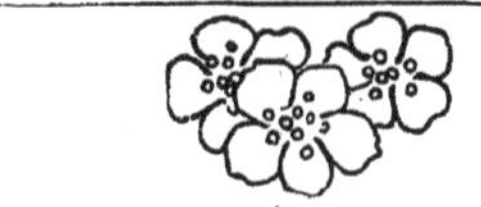

FIELD POPPY.

Materials required :—

1. Three squares of red tissue paper, two of 4 ins., one of 5 ins.
2. A yard of black unravelled wool.
3. Length of wire of 12 ins. for stem.
4. A piece of green paper 2 ins. by 1 in. for calyx.
5. A slip of green paper 7 ins. by $\frac{1}{2}$ in. for stem.

Method of preparing Paper.—This flower is made from squares of paper of two sizes, the larger being 5 ins. square and the smaller 4 ins. square.

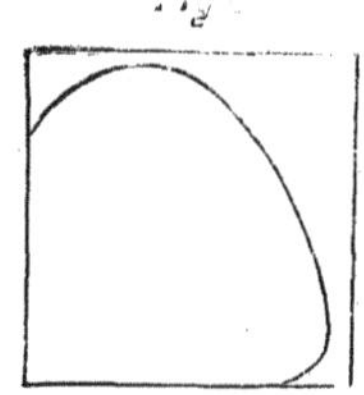

Each square is folded into four, point to point. Beginning about $\frac{1}{4}$ inch down each side, curve round each side and top. (Fig. 1.)

Creasing Petals.—Take hold of the corner of the square in the right hand, and draw in creases between

the third and fourth fingers of the left hand. Squeeze firmly, open out. Again without folding, draw through fingers twice again, still holding from the middle. The result of this is shown in Fig. 2. Each square is treated in this manner, one large square and two small ones being required for one flower.

Centre.—This is formed from black unravelled knitting wool, and is arranged in the same way as for Marguerite Daisies. (Fig. 3.)

Arrangement of Flower.—Thread one of small squares on to wire attached to centre, and again another square of petals, so that the second petals fall between those of the first. Place the large petals in the same way.

Calyx.—This is formed by folding stiff paper round the stem close to the petals, and fastening with gum, or by twisting one of the ends of wire round once or twice.

Cover calyx with green paper, about 1 in. wide, and twist a narrow piece round the wire for stem.

CORN FLOWER.

Materials required :—

1. A strip of blue tissue paper 1½ ins. by 12 ins.
2. A length of wire 18 ins. for stamens, with same length of brown tissue paper ½ in. wide, or,
   A piece of brown or black crêpe paper 2 ins. by 1½ ins. cut into fringes and twisted.
3. A strip of wire 12 ins. long for stem.
4. A piece of green tissue paper 2 ins. by 1 in. for calyx.
5. A strip of green tissue paper 7 ins. by ½ in. for stem.

Method of preparing Paper.—Centre.—The centre is formed of five or six pieces of wire, 3 ins. in length, and knotted at the top, covered with a narrow strip of brown paper twisted evenly over. (Fig. 1.)

A piece of brown paper, 2 ins. by 1 in., is fringed finely, and twisted round the central stamens. (Fig. 2.)

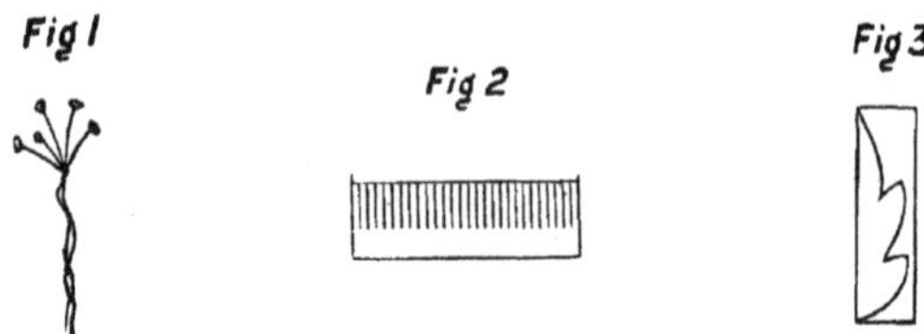

Petals.—Each petal requires to be separate and not attached to others, as in most flowers. A good many may, however, be cut together, and threaded separately.

Take a strip of any length and 1½ ins. in width. Fold till about 1½ ins. by 1 in. From top left hand corner curve down about half way. Form the remainder into two leaves like the common pattern of acanthus foliage (Fig. 3), taking care to keep them very narrow.

Arrangement of Flower.—About one dozen will be required for each flower, which must be threaded on a piece of wire, the petals still remaining folded. Each one must, however, be threaded separately. The wire will act as a gathering thread, which must be made to draw round the centre stamens, and twisted to attach it firmly. The remainder of wire is twisted to form stem.

Finish off the stem by twisting on a narrow strip of green paper. Arrange petals evenly round flower.

SWEET PEA.

Materials required :—

1. A piece of white tissue paper 3 ins. by 2 ins.
2. A piece of yellow tissue paper 3 ins. by 2 ins.
3. A piece of pink tissue paper 3 ins. by 2 ins.
4. A length of wire 8 ins. for stem.
5. A length of wire 6 ins. for tendril.
6. A piece of green tissue paper 8 ins. by ½ in. for stem, 6 ins. by ½ in. for tendril.
7. A piece of green crêpe paper 4½ ins. by 1½ ins. for leaves.

Method of Preparation.—This flower is made from three strips of paper, each 3 ins. by 2 ins., one each of pink, yellow, and white, or whatever colour the flower is to be.

These strips must all be put together and doubled, forming oblong 2 ins. by 1½ ins. With the double fold to left hand, curve off the top corner on the right (Fig. 1), keeping half the top quite straight.

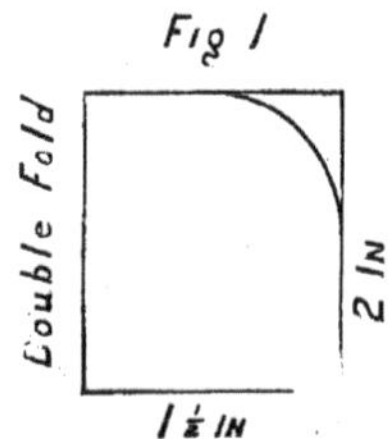

Take one piece for centre—in this case the yellow piece—leaving it doubled as before, gather in the fingers the bottom cut edges and half the cut edges of one side. Attach with wire of about 8 ins. length. (Fig. 2.)

Petals.—The pink paper is now needed. Gather this in the same manner, but this time only the bottom cut edges, and just catching in a little of one side. (Fig. 3.) It will be seen that the open edges of petals are put to the double fold of centre.

Fig. 2.

Fig. 3.

The outer petal is put on in the same way, and fastened by wire twisted round, it being gathered only at the bottom, and the outer edges turned back a little.

Mounting.—Stem.—Cover the stem with green tissue paper, fold it several times at top part nearest the

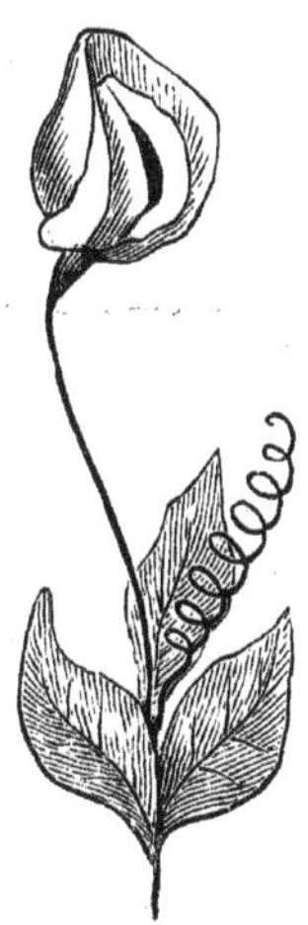

flower. Bend the stem about $\frac{1}{2}$ in. from flower, as in the case of the Daffodil. Continue wrapping stem.

Tendrils.—These are formed from a length of wire covered with green tissue paper as for a stem. The covered wire is now twisted round a pencil. This, when curled, is attached to the stem about 4 ins. from flower.

Two, three, or four flowers with one tendril may be attached to one stalk.

Leaves.—Three leaves may be cut from green crinkled paper, and arranged round the point of connection. These are of the ordinary shape and may be cut from a square $1\frac{1}{2}$ ins.

The stem below the point where all are joined must again be covered with green paper, and finished with a touch of gum.

PASSION FLOWER.

Materials required :—

1. Length of wire of 12 ins. for centre.
2. A strip of brown tissue paper 12 ins. by $\frac{1}{2}$ in.
3. A circle of purple tissue paper $1\frac{1}{4}$ ins., and one of $\frac{3}{4}$ in. radius.
4. A circle of white tissue paper $\frac{3}{4}$ in. radius.
5. A circle of green tissue paper $\frac{3}{4}$ in. radius.
6. Two strips of white crêpe paper 5 ins. long for petals.
7. One strip of green crêpe paper 5 ins. long for sepals.
8. Needle and thread.
9. Length of wire for stem 7 ins.
10. Length of green tissue paper 7 ins. by $\frac{1}{2}$ in. for stem.

Centre of Flower.—The centre of the flower is formed from three pieces of wire, 4ins. in length. The wire is doubled three or four times at one end to form a flat top of about $\frac{3}{8}$ in. Over the top and whole length of wire is twisted a narrow strip of brown paper. The three are twisted together at the bottom, and separated a little towards the top. (Fig. 1.) The next to be cut are one purple circle of $1\frac{1}{4}$ in. radius, and one each

Fig. 1.

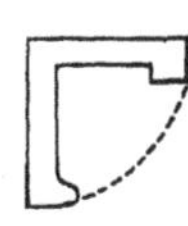

Fig. 2.

purple and white circles of $\frac{3}{4}$ in. radius. The two latter may be cut together, and all three finely fringed round edges almost to centre.

An extra green circle is required $\frac{3}{4}$ in. radius, which is folded in four, and cut in the form of a maltese cross with rounded corners. (Fig. 2.)

Petals.—The petals are cut from two strips of white and one of green crêpe paper of 5 ins. in length. These must be folded into six; and from the top centre point curved down each side three-fourths of the length. (Fig. 3.) Open out each length. Take the length of green petals, and place a length of white ones exactly

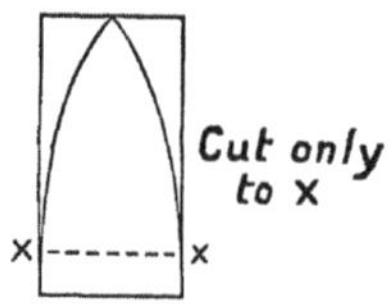

Fig. 3.

above. The remaining white petals are placed so that one white petal falls between the white ones of the layer beneath. Gather the three layers together along the lower edge.

Arrangement of Flower.—Take the centre (Fig. 1) and thread on to extended stem the cross of green paper.

Now one small purple and white fringe is threaded, and finally large purple fringe.

The petals which have been gathered together are now placed round stem beneath fringes, the gathering thread drawn up, twisted round, and fastened off securely.

Twist strip of green paper round wire for stem. The petals and centre will now require flattening a little, and arranging evenly.

When finished each petal should be taken hold of in the centre with thumb and finger, and drawing gently up to the tip of petal, curved in towards centre of flower. This opens out the paper in the centre without affecting the sides of petals.

REMARKS.

All these flowers look very effective if arranged with dried ferns, the common oak fern, or maiden-hair, or they may be mixed with dried grasses.

The outlay for this occupation is very trifling, and good sums of money may be gained by the sale of small bunches for a few pence.

The Daisies, Cornflowers, and other small flowers look very well arranged with fern and placed in small pots filled with moist clay and covered with green dried moss. These are suitable for table decoration in winter.

www.ingramcontent.com/pod-product-compliance
Ingram Content Group UK Ltd.
Pitfield, Milton Keynes, MK11 3LW, UK
UKHW042012190726
13854UKWH00005B/2266

9 781528 700269